S

Trails

D0825471

≈
The
Postcard
Archive
Series
≈

MUSEUM OF NEW MEXICO PRESS, SANTA FE, NEW MEXICO

T 107707

A note to the purchaser: The postcards in this book are slightly larger
than standard and require the same postage as first-class mail.

ISBN 0–89013–274-7.

Manufactured in Korea.
10 9 8 7 6 5 4 3 2 1

Design by Deborah Fleig.

Cover: **Bob Ervine with Santa Fe children on burro**, c. 1913.
     Photo by Jesse L. Nusbaum. MNM 117753.

Museum of New Mexico Press
P.O. Box 2087
Santa Fe, NM 87504

Preface

Richard Rudisill, Curator of Photographic History, Museum of New Mexico

The Historical Society of New Mexico began collecting pictures soon after its founding in 1859 with catalogue accessions including "Two Photographic views of the Washington Aqueduct" and "An ambrotype of José Calixto Borrego the Mexican dwarf." Although these initial pieces vanished in the disruption of the Civil War, the rebirth of the society in 1880 began steady growth of a collection which was assigned to the Museum of New Mexico in 1977. Since then, overall holdings have reached to half a million items. Subject-matter filing allows researchers to look as much as fourteen decades into New Mexico's past, to view buildings and spaces of Santa Fe or various pueblos, to see past dress styles or work actions, to meet face-to-face the people of earlier days, and to perceive the large and small changes in life otherwise unreachable or forgotten.

Many of these views were made by professionals, upon request or for their own reasons, as entertainment or postcards, for publication or sale. A great number came about simply as personal responses to family events and daily lives that elicted a wish to keep bits of them permanent or to share details with others. A remarkable aspect of the entire collection is that drastic changes in physical circumstances have not been matched by equal shift in the attitudes people hold about why they make pictures or why they enjoy them. Methods of scholarship or social conditions may fluctuate, but most people go on wanting to see how they or their predecessors have appeared and what remains recognizable from a time before. Nostalgia weighs as much as scholarship in such scales of appreciation.

Through its later history, New Mexico stayed current with general photographic practice. By the 1860s and '70s, a few of the studios in the territory were capable of issuing the popular stereoscopic views or producing sunlight enlargements equal with work from "the States." With the advent of the railroad and greater attention from anthropologists, artists, tourists, and traders, the materials and techniques of contemporary eastern work were to be had in Santa Fe or Las Vegas or New Albuquerque, and several major people worked or lived in the region. Ben Wittick, John K. Hillers, Willilam Henry Jackson, and Dana B. Chase were among them.

In the thirty years before World War I, Charles Lummis made hundreds of iron-base blueprints of Indian life, Adam Clark Vroman wrought images in platinum, Aaron Craycraft lugged an 8"x10" view camera into Frijoles Canyon and introduced Dr. Edgar Hewett (archaeologist and founder of the Museum of New Mexico) to the now-famous Tyuonyi Ruins, and Jesse Nusbaum pictured the architecture and rural details of northern New Mexico before recording the new museum's clearing of the Maya site of Quirigua in Guatemala and then going on to carry Pueblo-style structures into the 1915 Panama-California Exposition in San Diego. Then, and later, T. Harmon Parkhurst, H.F. Robinson, and Wesley Bradfield created arrays of negatives reflecting changes in town and Pueblo Indian life. Throughout all that time, amateurs were busy recording whatever the professionals missed to a degree that allows today's Museum of New Mexico Photo Archives to show the richly alive visual heritage of New Mexico.

The
Postcard
Archive
Series

From **Santa Fe Trails**, © 1995 MUSEUM OF NEW MEXICO PRESS, SANTA FE

Railroad Depot, Silver City, NM, c. 1915-20. MNM 51077.

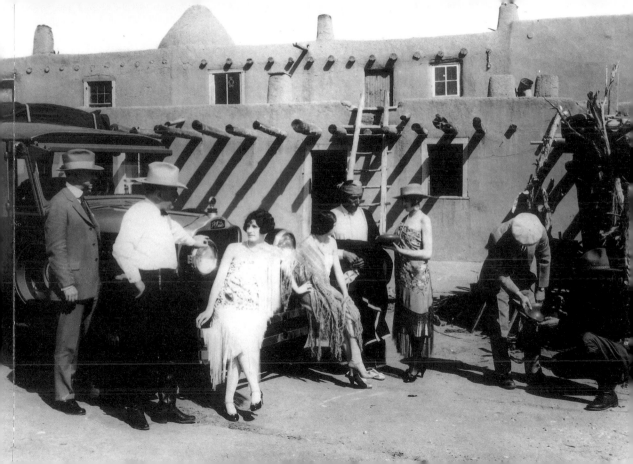

The Postcard Archive Series

From **Santa Fe Trails**. © 1995 MUSEUM OF NEW MEXICO PRESS, SANTA FE

Indian detour bus, Tesuque Pueblo, NM, c. 1930.
Photo by T. Harmon Parkhurst. MNM 132440.

The Postcard Archive Series

From **Santa Fe Trails.** © 1995 MUSEUM OF NEW MEXICO PRESS, SANTA FE

La Bajada road, New Mexico, c. 1913.
Photo by Jesse L. Nusbaum. MNM 118439.

The
Postcard
Archive
Series

Mrs. Small's Auto Party, Santa Fe, NM, 1912.
Photo by Jesse L. Nusbaum. MNM 61641.

Boy on burro with his dog, Kingston, NM,
c. 1885-92. Photo by J. C. Burge. MNM 76591.

The
Postcard
Archive
Series

AT&SF depot, Lamy, NM, 1937. MNM 142776.

≈
The
Postcard
Archive
Series
≈

From **Santa Fe Trails.** © 1995 MUSEUM OF NEW MEXICO PRESS, SANTA FE

Pulling car out of the mud, Chaco Canyon,
NM, 1931. Photo by Sam Hudelson. MNM 46486.

The Postcard Archive Series

From **Santa Fe Trails.** © 1995 MUSEUM OF NEW MEXICO PRESS, SANTA FE

Cycling men, New Mexico, 1885.
Photo by Dana B. Chase. MNM 2267.

The
Postcard
Archive
Series

From **Santa Fe Trails**. © 1995 MUSEUM OF NEW MEXICO PRESS, SANTA FE

Wagon Train, New Mexico, c. 1935.
Photo by T. Harmon Parkhurst. MNM 12014.

The
Postcard
Archive
Series

Logan Bridge, dedicated February 21, 1922,
Logan, NM. Photo by J. W. Farmer. MNM 145576.

The
Postcard
Archive
Series

From **Santa Fe Trails**, © 1995 MUSEUM OF NEW MEXICO PRESS, SANTA FE

Harvey Indian Detour bus, c. 1927. MNM 44426.

The
Postcard
Archive
Series

From **Santa Fe Trails.** © 1995 MUSEUM OF NEW MEXICO PRESS, SANTA FE

Costumed children in a pony cart,
Las Vegas, NM, c. 1898. MNM 77380.

The
Postcard
Archive
Series

Water Street at Galisteo,
Santa Fe, NM, c. 1900-05. MNM 11396.

The
Postcard
Archive
Series

Children in their burro cart, Santa Fe, NM, 1912. Photo by Jesse L. Nusbaum. MNM 61818.

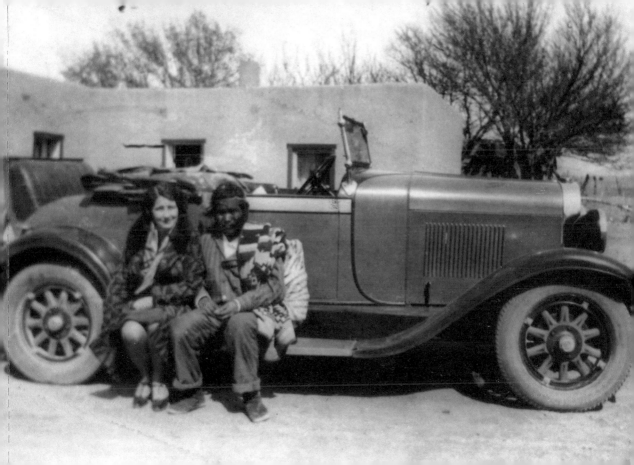

From **Santa Fe Trails.** © 1995 MUSEUM OF NEW MEXICO PRESS, SANTA FE

**Pueblo man posing with a woman
and her car**, New Mexico. MNM 151448.

≈

The
Postcard
Archive
Series

≈

From **Santa Fe Trails**, © 1995 MUSEUM OF NEW MEXICO PRESS, SANTA FE

Indian detour cars at AT&SF depot, Lamy, NM,
c. 1930. Photo by Edward A. Kemp. MNM 53651.

The
Postcard
Archive
Series

From **Santa Fe Trails.** © 1995 MUSEUM OF NEW MEXICO PRESS, SANTA FE

"New Mexico's Fairest," Nara Vista, NM. MNM 158309.

The
Postcard
Archive
Series

Some of the first cars in Raton in front
of the Seaberg Hotel, Raton, NM. MNM 14787.

The
Postcard
Archive
Series

From **Santa Fe Trails.** © 1995 MUSEUM OF NEW MEXICO PRESS, SANTA FE

AT&SF depot, Santa Fe, NM. MNM 104466.

The
Postcard
Archive
Series

Bridge Street, looking east,
Las Vegas, NM, 1892. MNM 14720.

The
Postcard
Archive
Series

Children and burro, Las Vegas, NM, 1898. MNM 76980.

AT&SF depot, Santa Fe, NM, 1908.
Photo by Jesse L. Nusbaum. MNM 66658.

The
Postcard
Archive
Series

Wagon ruts along the Santa Fe Trail, near Fort Union, NM. Photo by Harold D. Walter. MNM 128726.

La Fonda Hotel decorated for Christmas, Santa Fe,
NM, c. 1935. Photo by T. Harmon Parkhurst. MNM 54311.

The Chic-ito automobile, designed by Leopold E. Garcia
of NM, c. 1956. Photo by E.W. Northnagel. MNM 127466.

The
Postcard
Archive
Series

Bob Ervine with Santa Fe children on burro,
c. 1913. Photo by Jesse L. Nusbaum. MNM 117753.

The
Postcard
Archive
Series

From **Santa Fe Trails.** © 1995 MUSEUM OF NEW MEXICO PRESS, SANTA FE

La Bajada road, New Mexico, c. 1930.
Photo by T. Harmon Parkhurst. MNM 31166.

The
Postcard
Archive
Series

From **Santa Fe Trails.** © 1995 MUSEUM OF NEW MEXICO PRESS, SANTA FE

Burro-pulled wagon, New Mexico, c. 1935.
Photo by T. Harmon Parkhurst. MNM 12020.

≈

The
Postcard
Archive
Series

≈

From **Santa Fe Trails**, © 1995 MUSEUM OF NEW MEXICO PRESS, SANTA FE

Railroad Depot, Silver City, NM, c. 1915-20.
Photo by Waldo Twitchell. MNM 51083.

The
Postcard
Archive
Series

The portal of the Palace of the Governors, Santa Fe, NM, c. 1928. Photo by T. Harmon Parkhurst. MNM 10598.